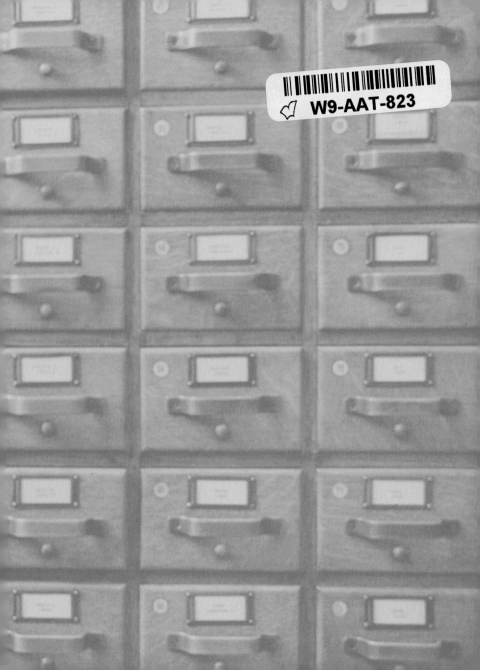

W9-AAT-823

THIS READING JOURNAL BELONGS TO:

Read in order to live.

—Gustave Flaubert

POTTER STYLE · DESIGN BY LAURA PALESE · Cover photography credits: Bookshelf © Júliá Runólfsdóttir/Flickr/Getty Images; Card Catalog © Reza Estakhrian/ Stone+/Getty Images; Typewriter © Veer Incorporated. Copyright © 2010 by Potter Style. · All rights reserved. Published in the United States by Potter Style, an imprint of the Crown Publishing Group, a division of Random House, Inc., New York. · www.clarksonpotter.com · 978-0-307-59166-1 · Printed in China

Beginning a new book is one of the most simple yet exciting pleasures in life. And finishing a good book is even more satisfying.

Use this journal to keep track of all the books you've read and plan to read next. If you're looking for guidance or want to know what the experts recommend, refer to the numerous lists in the back of this journal for easy inspiration. You'll find checklists of award-winning novels, notable books, and genre-specific favorites. Never again will you have to ask yourself, "What should I read next?" Make sure to cross off any titles you've completed when you're done.

As you fill out the entry pages in this journal, you'll come across interactive prompts to supplement your reading experience. Answer questions about your literary preferences, cast your own movie adaptation of a favorite book, record noteworthy passages or quotes, and plan a literary pilgrimage. You can also use the pages in the back of the journal to record any author readings you've attended, list bookstore contact information, and keep track of any books you've borrowed or loaned.

This journal offers a novel way to file your bibliophilic notes and makes an ideal companion for book lovers. Happy reading!

TITLE: _____

AUTHOR: _____

DATE PUBLISHED: _____

CATEGORY: ☐ FICTION ☐ NONFICTION ☐ MEMOIR

☐ BIOGRAPHY ☐ OTHER _____

DATE STARTED: _____ DATE FINISHED: _____

RATING: ☆ ☆ ☆ ☆ ☆

INSPIRED ME TO LEARN ABOUT THESE SUBJECTS: _____

_____

_____

_____

_____

_____

_____

_____

_____

_____

_____

_____

TITLE: _____

AUTHOR: _____

DATE PUBLISHED: _____

CATEGORY: ☐ FICTION ☐ NONFICTION ☐ MEMOIR

☐ BIOGRAPHY ☐ OTHER _____

DATE STARTED: _____ DATE FINISHED: _____

RATING: ☆ ☆ ☆ ☆ ☆

INSPIRED ME TO LEARN ABOUT THESE SUBJECTS: _____

_____

_____

_____

_____

_____

_____

_____

_____

_____

_____

_____

_____

She is too fond of books, and it has turned her brain.
—Louisa May Alcott

TITLE: _____

AUTHOR: _____

DATE PUBLISHED: _____

CATEGORY: ☐ FICTION ☐ NONFICTION ☐ MEMOIR

           ☐ BIOGRAPHY ☐ OTHER _____

DATE STARTED: _____ DATE FINISHED: _____

RATING: ☆ ☆ ☆ ☆ ☆

INSPIRED ME TO LEARN ABOUT THESE SUBJECTS: _____

_____

_____

_____

_____

_____

_____

_____

_____

_____

_____

_____

_____

TITLE: _____

AUTHOR: _____

DATE PUBLISHED: _____

CATEGORY: ☐ FICTION ☐ NONFICTION ☐ MEMOIR

☐ BIOGRAPHY ☐ OTHER _____

DATE STARTED: _____ DATE FINISHED: _____

RATING: ☆ ☆ ☆ ☆ ☆

INSPIRED ME TO LEARN ABOUT THESE SUBJECTS: _____

_____

_____

_____

_____

_____

_____

_____

_____

_____

_____

_____

_____

TITLE: _____

AUTHOR: _____

DATE PUBLISHED: _____

CATEGORY: ☐ FICTION ☐ NONFICTION ☐ MEMOIR

           ☐ BIOGRAPHY ☐ OTHER _____

DATE STARTED: _____ DATE FINISHED: _____

RATING: ☆ ☆ ☆ ☆ ☆

INSPIRED ME TO LEARN ABOUT THESE SUBJECTS: _____

_____

_____

_____

_____

_____

_____

_____

_____

_____

_____

_____

MY BIBLIO STYLE

CURRENT FAVORITE AUTHORS

CURRENT FAVORITE BOOKS ————————————————————

FAVORITE YOUNG ADULT BOOKS

_____

_____

_____

_____

FAVORITE CHILDHOOD BOOKS

_____

_____

_____

_____

MY FAVORITE PLACES TO READ
(check all that apply)

☐ in a café

☐ at home

☐ at the beach

☐ at a library

☐ on a train

☐ on an airplane

☐ in the park

☐ in bed

MY READING SPEED

☐ slow and steady wins the race

☐ not too fast, not too slow—just right

☐ jack be nimble, jack be quick

MY FAVORITE GENRES
(check all that apply)

☐ adventure

☐ autobiography/biography

☐ classics

☐ contemporary fiction

☐ drama/plays

☐ graphic novels

☐ historical fiction

☐ horror

☐ humor

☐ mysteries/detective fiction

☐ romance

☐ science fiction

☐ travel

TITLE: _____

AUTHOR: _____

DATE PUBLISHED: _____

CATEGORY: ☐ FICTION ☐ NONFICTION ☐ MEMOIR

☐ BIOGRAPHY ☐ OTHER _____

DATE STARTED: _____ DATE FINISHED: _____

RATING: ☆ ☆ ☆ ☆ ☆

INSPIRED ME TO LEARN ABOUT THESE SUBJECTS: _____

_____

_____

_____

_____

_____

_____

_____

_____

_____

_____

_____

TITLE: _____

AUTHOR: _____

DATE PUBLISHED: _____

CATEGORY: ☐ FICTION ☐ NONFICTION ☐ MEMOIR

          ☐ BIOGRAPHY ☐ OTHER _____

DATE STARTED: _____ DATE FINISHED: _____

RATING: ☆ ☆ ☆ ☆ ☆

INSPIRED ME TO LEARN ABOUT THESE SUBJECTS: _____

_____

_____

_____

_____

_____

_____

_____

_____

_____

_____

_____

_____

It is a great thing to start life with a small number of really good books which are your very own.

—Sir Arthur Conan Doyle

TITLE: _____

AUTHOR: _____

DATE PUBLISHED: _____

CATEGORY: ☐ FICTION ☐ NONFICTION ☐ MEMOIR

           ☐ BIOGRAPHY ☐ OTHER _____

DATE STARTED: _____ DATE FINISHED: _____

RATING: ☆ ☆ ☆ ☆ ☆

INSPIRED ME TO LEARN ABOUT THESE SUBJECTS: _____

_____

_____

_____

_____

_____

_____

_____

_____

_____

_____

_____

_____

_____

TITLE: _____

AUTHOR: _____

DATE PUBLISHED: _____

CATEGORY: ☐ FICTION ☐ NONFICTION ☐ MEMOIR

          ☐ BIOGRAPHY ☐ OTHER _____

DATE STARTED: _____ DATE FINISHED: _____

RATING: ☆ ☆ ☆ ☆ ☆

INSPIRED ME TO LEARN ABOUT THESE SUBJECTS: _____

_____

_____

_____

_____

_____

_____

_____

_____

_____

_____

_____

_____

_____

TITLE: _____

AUTHOR: _____

DATE PUBLISHED: _____

CATEGORY: ☐ FICTION ☐ NONFICTION ☐ MEMOIR

☐ BIOGRAPHY ☐ OTHER _____

DATE STARTED: _____ DATE FINISHED: _____

RATING: ☆ ☆ ☆ ☆ ☆

INSPIRED ME TO LEARN ABOUT THESE SUBJECTS: _____

_____

_____

_____

_____

_____

_____

_____

_____

_____

_____

_____

_____

_____

SHELF LIFE

Genres that currently occupy my shelves. Shade in the amount.

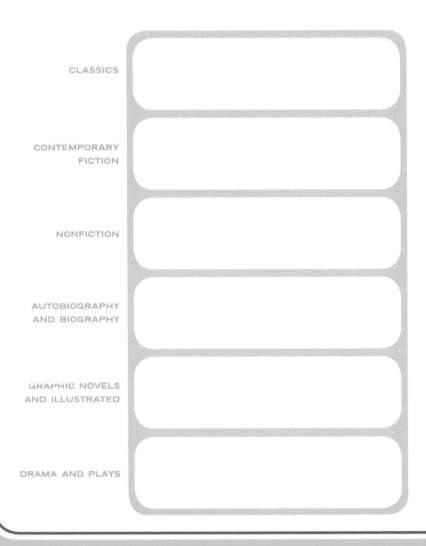

CLASSICS

CONTEMPORARY
FICTION

NONFICTION

AUTOBIOGRAPHY
AND BIOGRAPHY

GRAPHIC NOVELS
AND ILLUSTRATED

DRAMA AND PLAYS

Authors that have
most influenced me.

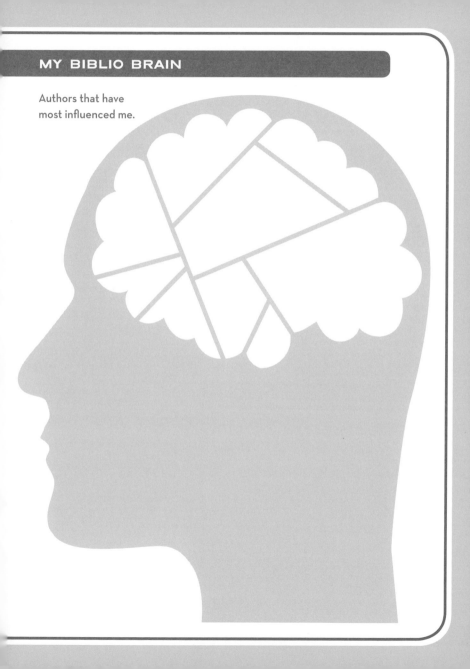

TITLE: _____

AUTHOR: _____

DATE PUBLISHED: _____

CATEGORY: ☐ FICTION ☐ NONFICTION ☐ MEMOIR

☐ BIOGRAPHY ☐ OTHER _____

DATE STARTED: _____ DATE FINISHED: _____

RATING: ☆ ☆ ☆ ☆ ☆

INSPIRED ME TO LEARN ABOUT THESE SUBJECTS: _____

_____

_____

_____

_____

_____

_____

_____

_____

_____

_____

_____

_____

TITLE: _____

AUTHOR: _____

DATE PUBLISHED: _____

CATEGORY: ☐ FICTION ☐ NONFICTION ☐ MEMOIR

☐ BIOGRAPHY ☐ OTHER _____

DATE STARTED: _____ DATE FINISHED: _____

RATING: ☆ ☆ ☆ ☆ ☆

INSPIRED ME TO LEARN ABOUT THESE SUBJECTS: _____

_____

_____

_____

_____

_____

_____

_____

_____

_____

_____

_____

_____

Books—the children of the brain.
—Jonathan Swift

TITLE: _____

AUTHOR: _____

DATE PUBLISHED: _____

CATEGORY: ☐ FICTION ☐ NONFICTION ☐ MEMOIR

☐ BIOGRAPHY ☐ OTHER _____

DATE STARTED: _____ DATE FINISHED: _____

RATING: ☆ ☆ ☆ ☆ ☆

INSPIRED ME TO LEARN ABOUT THESE SUBJECTS: _____

_____

_____

_____

_____

_____

_____

_____

_____

_____

_____

_____

_____

_____

_____

TITLE: _____

AUTHOR: _____

DATE PUBLISHED: _____

CATEGORY: ☐ FICTION ☐ NONFICTION ☐ MEMOIR

             ☐ BIOGRAPHY ☐ OTHER _____

DATE STARTED: _____ DATE FINISHED: _____

RATING: ☆ ☆ ☆ ☆ ☆

INSPIRED ME TO LEARN ABOUT THESE SUBJECTS: _____

_____

_____

_____

_____

_____

_____

_____

_____

_____

_____

_____

_____

TITLE: _____

AUTHOR: _____

DATE PUBLISHED: _____

CATEGORY: ☐ FICTION ☐ NONFICTION ☐ MEMOIR

☐ BIOGRAPHY ☐ OTHER _____

DATE STARTED: _____ DATE FINISHED: _____

RATING: ☆ ☆ ☆ ☆ ☆

INSPIRED ME TO LEARN ABOUT THESE SUBJECTS: _____

_____

_____

_____

_____

_____

_____

_____

_____

_____

_____

_____

READING TREES

Made me want to learn more about these subjects

Made me want to read these other books by different authors

Made me want to read these other books by the same author

BOOK

Made me want to read these other books by different authors

Made me want to learn more about these subjects

BOOK

Made me want to read these other books by the same author

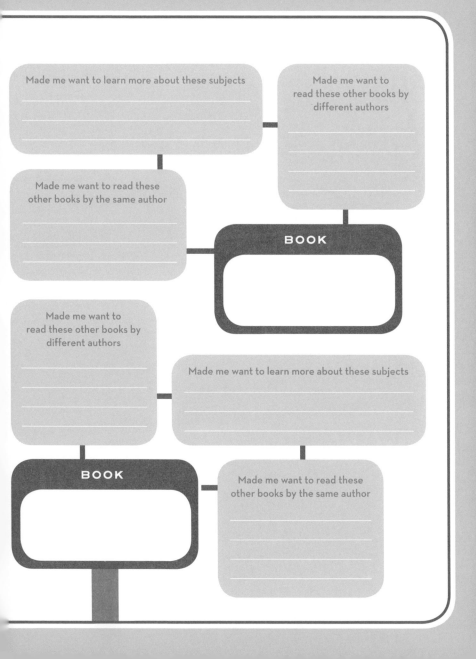

TITLE: _____

AUTHOR: _____

DATE PUBLISHED: _____

CATEGORY: ☐ FICTION ☐ NONFICTION ☐ MEMOIR

☐ BIOGRAPHY ☐ OTHER _____

DATE STARTED: _____ DATE FINISHED: _____

RATING: ☆ ☆ ☆ ☆ ☆

INSPIRED ME TO LEARN ABOUT THESE SUBJECTS: _____

_____

_____

_____

_____

_____

_____

_____

_____

_____

_____

_____

_____

_____

TITLE: _____

AUTHOR: _____

DATE PUBLISHED: _____

CATEGORY: ☐ FICTION ☐ NONFICTION ☐ MEMOIR

☐ BIOGRAPHY ☐ OTHER _____

DATE STARTED: _____ DATE FINISHED: _____

RATING: ☆ ☆ ☆ ☆ ☆

INSPIRED ME TO LEARN ABOUT THESE SUBJECTS: _____

_____

_____

_____

_____

_____

_____

_____

_____

_____

_____

_____

_____

Today a reader, tomorrow a leader.
—Margaret Fuller

TITLE: _____

AUTHOR: _____

DATE PUBLISHED: _____

CATEGORY: ☐ FICTION ☐ NONFICTION ☐ MEMOIR

☐ BIOGRAPHY ☐ OTHER _____

DATE STARTED: _____ DATE FINISHED: _____

RATING: ☆ ☆ ☆ ☆ ☆

INSPIRED ME TO LEARN ABOUT THESE SUBJECTS: _____

_____

_____

_____

_____

_____

_____

_____

_____

_____

_____

_____

_____

TITLE: _____

AUTHOR: _____

DATE PUBLISHED: _____

CATEGORY: ☐ FICTION ☐ NONFICTION ☐ MEMOIR

☐ BIOGRAPHY ☐ OTHER _____

DATE STARTED: _____ DATE FINISHED: _____

RATING: ☆ ☆ ☆ ☆ ☆

INSPIRED ME TO LEARN ABOUT THESE SUBJECTS: _____

_____

_____

_____

_____

_____

_____

_____

_____

_____

_____

_____

_____

_____

TITLE: _____

AUTHOR: _____

DATE PUBLISHED: _____

CATEGORY: ☐ FICTION ☐ NONFICTION ☐ MEMOIR

☐ BIOGRAPHY ☐ OTHER _____

DATE STARTED: _____ DATE FINISHED: _____

RATING: ☆ ☆ ☆ ☆ ☆

INSPIRED ME TO LEARN ABOUT THESE SUBJECTS: _____

_____

_____

_____

_____

_____

_____

_____

_____

_____

_____

_____

LITERARY SUPERLATIVES

CHARACTERS MOST LIKE ME _____

_____

CHARACTERS I'D MOST WANT TO BE _____

_____

LITERARY CRUSHES _____

_____

_____   WITTIEST CHARACTER

BEST LITERARY CLOWNS _____

_____

BEST LITERARY MONSTERS _____

_____

MOST ROMANTIC LITERARY COUPLES _____

_____

_____

CHARACTERS I'D MOST WANT AS FRIENDS _____

_____

_____

CHARACTERS I WOULDN'T WANT AS ENEMIES _____

MOST
EXOTIC
SETTING
_____

PLACES IN BOOKS I MOST WANT TO VISIT _____

_____

_____

PLACES IN BOOKS I'D LEAST LIKE TO VISIT _____

_____

_____

CHARACTERS' WARDROBES I'D MOST WANT TO HAVE _____

_____

CHARACTERS' HOMES I'D MOST WANT TO LIVE IN _____

_____

BOOK THAT MADE ME THE MOST SCARED _____

_____

BOOK THAT MADE ME CRY THE MOST

_____

BOOK THAT MADE ME LAUGH THE MOST

_____

BOOK THAT MADE ME THE MOST BORED _____

_____

BOOK THAT MADE ME THE ANGRIEST _____

_____

BOOK I
LEARNED THE
MOST FROM

TITLE: _____

AUTHOR: _____

DATE PUBLISHED: _____

CATEGORY: ☐ FICTION ☐ NONFICTION ☐ MEMOIR

☐ BIOGRAPHY ☐ OTHER _____

DATE STARTED: _____ DATE FINISHED: _____

RATING: ☆ ☆ ☆ ☆ ☆

INSPIRED ME TO LEARN ABOUT THESE SUBJECTS: _____

_____

_____

_____

_____

_____

_____

_____

_____

_____

_____

_____

_____

TITLE: _____

AUTHOR: _____

DATE PUBLISHED: _____

CATEGORY: ☐ FICTION ☐ NONFICTION ☐ MEMOIR

☐ BIOGRAPHY ☐ OTHER _____

DATE STARTED: _____ DATE FINISHED: _____

RATING: ☆ ☆ ☆ ☆ ☆

INSPIRED ME TO LEARN ABOUT THESE SUBJECTS: _____

_____

_____

_____

_____

_____

_____

_____

_____

_____

_____

_____

_____

_____

I have always imagined that Paradise will be a kind of library.
—Jorge Luis Borges

TITLE: _____

AUTHOR: _____

DATE PUBLISHED: _____

CATEGORY: ☐ FICTION ☐ NONFICTION ☐ MEMOIR

☐ BIOGRAPHY ☐ OTHER _____

DATE STARTED: _____ DATE FINISHED: _____

RATING: ☆ ☆ ☆ ☆ ☆

INSPIRED ME TO LEARN ABOUT THESE SUBJECTS: _____

_____

_____

_____

_____

_____

_____

_____

_____

_____

_____

_____

_____

TITLE: _____

AUTHOR: _____

DATE PUBLISHED: _____

CATEGORY: ☐ FICTION ☐ NONFICTION ☐ MEMOIR

            ☐ BIOGRAPHY ☐ OTHER _____

DATE STARTED: _____ DATE FINISHED: _____

RATING: ☆ ☆ ☆ ☆ ☆

INSPIRED ME TO LEARN ABOUT THESE SUBJECTS: _____

_____

_____

_____

_____

_____

_____

_____

_____

_____

_____

_____

_____

_____

TITLE: _____

AUTHOR: _____

DATE PUBLISHED: _____

CATEGORY: ☐ FICTION ☐ NONFICTION ☐ MEMOIR

   ☐ BIOGRAPHY ☐ OTHER _____

DATE STARTED: _____ DATE FINISHED: _____

RATING: ☆ ☆ ☆ ☆ ☆

INSPIRED ME TO LEARN ABOUT THESE SUBJECTS: _____

_____

_____

_____

_____

_____

_____

_____

_____

_____

_____

_____

_____

_____

LITERARY PILGRIMAGES

These books make me want to visit these places:

BOOK	DESTINATION

MY FAVORITE BOOK SETTINGS INCLUDE _____

_____

_____

_____

_____

_____

_____

_____

_____

_____

MY FAVORITE INTERNATIONAL AUTHORS INCLUDE _____

_____

_____

_____

_____

_____

_____

_____

_____

_____

_____

_____

TITLE: _____

AUTHOR: _____

DATE PUBLISHED: _____

CATEGORY: ☐ FICTION ☐ NONFICTION ☐ MEMOIR

☐ BIOGRAPHY ☐ OTHER _____

DATE STARTED: _____ DATE FINISHED: _____

RATING: ☆ ☆ ☆ ☆ ☆

INSPIRED ME TO LEARN ABOUT THESE SUBJECTS: _____

_____

_____

_____

_____

_____

_____

_____

_____

_____

_____

_____

_____

_____

TITLE: _____

AUTHOR: _____

DATE PUBLISHED: _____

CATEGORY: ☐ FICTION ☐ NONFICTION ☐ MEMOIR

☐ BIOGRAPHY ☐ OTHER _____

DATE STARTED: _____ DATE FINISHED: _____

RATING: ☆ ☆ ☆ ☆ ☆

INSPIRED ME TO LEARN ABOUT THESE SUBJECTS: _____

_____

_____

_____

_____

_____

_____

_____

_____

_____

_____

_____

_____

_____

We read to know we are not alone.
—C.S. Lewis

TITLE: _____

AUTHOR: _____

DATE PUBLISHED: _____

CATEGORY: ☐ FICTION ☐ NONFICTION ☐ MEMOIR

☐ BIOGRAPHY ☐ OTHER _____

DATE STARTED: _____ DATE FINISHED: _____

RATING: ☆ ☆ ☆ ☆ ☆

INSPIRED ME TO LEARN ABOUT THESE SUBJECTS: _____

_____

_____

_____

_____

_____

_____

_____

_____

_____

_____

_____

_____

TITLE: _____

AUTHOR: _____

DATE PUBLISHED: _____

CATEGORY: ☐ FICTION ☐ NONFICTION ☐ MEMOIR

           ☐ BIOGRAPHY ☐ OTHER _____

DATE STARTED: _____ DATE FINISHED: _____

RATING: ☆ ☆ ☆ ☆ ☆

INSPIRED ME TO LEARN ABOUT THESE SUBJECTS: _____

_____

_____

_____

_____

_____

_____

_____

_____

_____

_____

_____

_____

_____

TITLE: _____

AUTHOR: _____

DATE PUBLISHED: _____

CATEGORY: ☐ FICTION ☐ NONFICTION ☐ MEMOIR

☐ BIOGRAPHY ☐ OTHER _____

DATE STARTED: _____ DATE FINISHED: _____

RATING: ☆ ☆ ☆ ☆ ☆

INSPIRED ME TO LEARN ABOUT THESE SUBJECTS: _____

_____

_____

_____

_____

_____

_____

_____

_____

_____

_____

_____

_____

_____

READING TREES

Made me want to learn more about these subjects

Made me want to
read these other books by
different authors

Made me want to read these
other books by the same author

BOOK

Made me want to
read these other books by
different authors

Made me want to learn more about these subjects

BOOK

Made me want to read these
other books by the same author

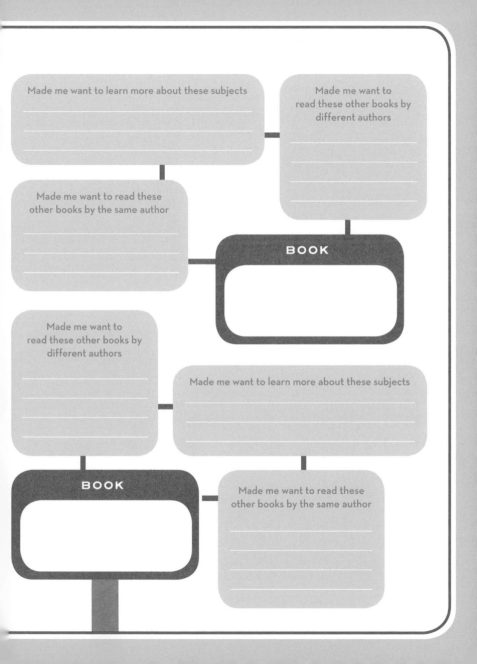

Made me want to learn more about these subjects

Made me want to read these other books by different authors

Made me want to read these other books by the same author

BOOK

Made me want to read these other books by different authors

Made me want to learn more about these subjects

BOOK

Made me want to read these other books by the same author

TITLE: _____

AUTHOR: _____

DATE PUBLISHED: _____

CATEGORY: ☐ FICTION ☐ NONFICTION ☐ MEMOIR

           ☐ BIOGRAPHY ☐ OTHER _____

DATE STARTED: _____ DATE FINISHED: _____

RATING: ☆ ☆ ☆ ☆ ☆

INSPIRED ME TO LEARN ABOUT THESE SUBJECTS: _____

_____

_____

_____

_____

_____

_____

_____

_____

_____

_____

_____

_____

_____

TITLE: _____

AUTHOR: _____

DATE PUBLISHED: _____

CATEGORY: ☐ FICTION ☐ NONFICTION ☐ MEMOIR

           ☐ BIOGRAPHY ☐ OTHER _____

DATE STARTED: _____ DATE FINISHED: _____

RATING: ☆ ☆ ☆ ☆ ☆

INSPIRED ME TO LEARN ABOUT THESE SUBJECTS: _____

_____

_____

_____

_____

_____

_____

_____

_____

_____

_____

_____

_____

Literature is my Utopia.
—Helen Keller

TITLE: _____

AUTHOR: _____

DATE PUBLISHED: _____

CATEGORY: ☐ FICTION ☐ NONFICTION ☐ MEMOIR

☐ BIOGRAPHY ☐ OTHER _____

DATE STARTED: _____ DATE FINISHED: _____

RATING: ☆ ☆ ☆ ☆ ☆

INSPIRED ME TO LEARN ABOUT THESE SUBJECTS: _____

_____

_____

_____

_____

_____

_____

_____

_____

_____

_____

_____

_____

TITLE: _____

AUTHOR: _____

DATE PUBLISHED: _____

CATEGORY: ☐ FICTION ☐ NONFICTION ☐ MEMOIR

☐ BIOGRAPHY ☐ OTHER _____

DATE STARTED: _____ DATE FINISHED: _____

RATING: ☆ ☆ ☆ ☆ ☆

INSPIRED ME TO LEARN ABOUT THESE SUBJECTS: _____

_____

_____

_____

_____

_____

_____

_____

_____

_____

_____

_____

_____

TITLE: _____

AUTHOR: _____

DATE PUBLISHED: _____

CATEGORY: ☐ FICTION ☐ NONFICTION ☐ MEMOIR

☐ BIOGRAPHY ☐ OTHER _____

DATE STARTED: _____ DATE FINISHED: _____

RATING: ☆ ☆ ☆ ☆ ☆

INSPIRED ME TO LEARN ABOUT THESE SUBJECTS: _____

_____

_____

_____

_____

_____

_____

_____

_____

_____

_____

_____

_____

_____

LITERARY FACE-OFFS

I PREFER:

☐ *The Odyssey*   vs. ☐ *The Iliad*

☐ Ernest Hemingway   vs. ☐ F. Scott Fitzgerald

☐ Charlotte Brontë   vs. ☐ Emily Brontë

☐ Elinor Dashwood   vs. ☐ Marianne Dashwood

☐ Kingsley Amis   vs. ☐ Martin Amis

☐ Sam Spade   vs. ☐ Philip Marlowe

☐ Ralph Ellison's *Invisible Man* vs. ☐ H. G. Wells's *The Invisible Man*

☐ *Dracula*   vs. ☐ *Frankenstein*

☐ Miss Marple   vs. ☐ Hercule Poirot

☐ Tom Sawyer   vs. ☐ Huckleberry Finn

☐ Mary Shelley   vs. ☐ Percy Bysshe Shelley

☐ Captain Ahab   vs. ☐ Captain Nemo

☐ Alice   vs. ☐ Dorothy

☐ Jack Kerouac   vs. ☐ Hunter S. Thompson

IF I WAS . . .

A LITTLE WOMAN, I'D BE:

☐ Amy

☐ Jo

☐ Meg

☐ Beth

A BROTHER KARAMAZOV, I'D BE:

☐ Alyosha

☐ Smerdyakov

☐ Dmitri

A JANE AUSTEN HEROINE, I'D BE:

☐ Elizabeth Bennet

☐ Fanny Price

☐ Marianne Dashwood

☐ Elinor Dashwood

☐ Catherine Morland

☐ Emma Woodhouse

☐ Anne Elliot

A SHAKESPEAREAN TRAGIC HERO, I'D BE:

☐ Hamlet

☐ King Lear

☐ Macbeth

☐ Othello

☐ Romeo

A MUSKETEER, I'D BE:

☐ Porthos

☐ Aramis

☐ Athos

☐ D'Artagnan

A LITERARY DOCTOR, I'D BE:

☐ Dr. Faustus

☐ Dr. Jekyll

☐ Dr. Victor Frankenstein

☐ Dr. Zhivago

☐ Dr. Moreau

A LITERARY TRAVELER, I'D VISIT:

☐ Narnia

☐ Lilliput

☐ Middle Earth

☐ Oz

☐ Never Never Land

A LITERARY DETECTIVE, I'D BE:

☐ Sherlock Holmes

☐ Hercule Poirot

☐ Jane Marple

☐ Auguste Dupin

☐ Philip Marlowe

☐ Lew Archer

☐ Lord Peter Whimsey

☐ Sam Spade

A LITERARY VILLAIN, I'D BE:

☐ Miss Havisham

☐ Professor Moriarty

☐ Count Dracula

☐ Grendel

☐ Iago

☐ Mr. Hyde

IN A LITERARY RELATIONSHIP, IT WOULD BE MOST LIKE:

☐ Rhett and Scarlet

☐ Romeo and Juliet

☐ Elizabeth Bennet and Mr. Darcy

☐ Jay Gatsby and Daisy Buchanan

☐ Catherine and Heathcliff

TITLE: _____

AUTHOR: _____

DATE PUBLISHED: _____

CATEGORY: ☐ FICTION ☐ NONFICTION ☐ MEMOIR

☐ BIOGRAPHY ☐ OTHER _____

DATE STARTED: _____ DATE FINISHED: _____

RATING: ☆ ☆ ☆ ☆ ☆

INSPIRED ME TO LEARN ABOUT THESE SUBJECTS: _____

_____

_____

_____

_____

_____

_____

_____

_____

_____

_____

_____

_____

_____

TITLE: _____

AUTHOR: _____

DATE PUBLISHED: _____

CATEGORY: ☐ FICTION ☐ NONFICTION ☐ MEMOIR

☐ BIOGRAPHY ☐ OTHER _____

DATE STARTED: _____ DATE FINISHED: _____

RATING: ☆ ☆ ☆ ☆ ☆

INSPIRED ME TO LEARN ABOUT THESE SUBJECTS: _____

_____

_____

_____

_____

_____

_____

_____

_____

_____

_____

_____

_____

Where is human nature so weak as in the bookstore?
—Henry Ward Beecher

TITLE: _____

AUTHOR: _____

DATE PUBLISHED: _____

CATEGORY: ☐ FICTION ☐ NONFICTION ☐ MEMOIR

☐ BIOGRAPHY ☐ OTHER _____

DATE STARTED: _____ DATE FINISHED: _____

RATING: ☆ ☆ ☆ ☆ ☆

INSPIRED ME TO LEARN ABOUT THESE SUBJECTS: _____

_____

_____

_____

_____

_____

_____

_____

_____

_____

_____

_____

_____

_____

TITLE: _____

AUTHOR: _____

DATE PUBLISHED: _____

CATEGORY: ☐ FICTION ☐ NONFICTION ☐ MEMOIR

☐ BIOGRAPHY ☐ OTHER _____

DATE STARTED: _____ DATE FINISHED: _____

RATING: ☆ ☆ ☆ ☆ ☆

INSPIRED ME TO LEARN ABOUT THESE SUBJECTS: _____

_____

_____

_____

_____

_____

_____

_____

_____

_____

_____

_____

_____

_____

TITLE: _____

AUTHOR: _____

DATE PUBLISHED: _____

CATEGORY: ☐ FICTION ☐ NONFICTION ☐ MEMOIR

☐ BIOGRAPHY ☐ OTHER _____

DATE STARTED: _____ DATE FINISHED: _____

RATING: ☆ ☆ ☆ ☆ ☆

INSPIRED ME TO LEARN ABOUT THESE SUBJECTS: _____

_____

_____

_____

_____

_____

_____

_____

_____

_____

_____

_____

_____

_____

Some of my favorite quotes or passages:

"_____
_____
_____
_____"

"_____
_____
_____
_____"

"_____
_____
_____
_____
_____
_____"

TITLE: _____

AUTHOR: _____

DATE PUBLISHED: _____

CATEGORY: ☐ FICTION ☐ NONFICTION ☐ MEMOIR

☐ BIOGRAPHY ☐ OTHER _____

DATE STARTED: _____ DATE FINISHED: _____

RATING: ☆ ☆ ☆ ☆ ☆

INSPIRED ME TO LEARN ABOUT THESE SUBJECTS: _____

_____

_____

_____

_____

_____

_____

_____

_____

_____

_____

_____

_____

_____

TITLE: _____

AUTHOR: _____

DATE PUBLISHED: _____

CATEGORY: ☐ FICTION ☐ NONFICTION ☐ MEMOIR

☐ BIOGRAPHY ☐ OTHER _____

DATE STARTED: _____ DATE FINISHED: _____

RATING: ☆ ☆ ☆ ☆ ☆

INSPIRED ME TO LEARN ABOUT THESE SUBJECTS: _____

_____

_____

_____

_____

_____

_____

_____

_____

_____

_____

_____

_____

_____

A room without books is like a body without a soul.
—Cicero

TITLE: _____

AUTHOR: _____

DATE PUBLISHED: _____

CATEGORY: ☐ FICTION ☐ NONFICTION ☐ MEMOIR

☐ BIOGRAPHY ☐ OTHER _____

DATE STARTED: _____ DATE FINISHED: _____

RATING: ☆ ☆ ☆ ☆ ☆

INSPIRED ME TO LEARN ABOUT THESE SUBJECTS: _____

_____

_____

_____

_____

_____

_____

_____

_____

_____

_____

_____

_____

_____

TITLE: _____

AUTHOR: _____

DATE PUBLISHED: _____

CATEGORY: ☐ FICTION ☐ NONFICTION ☐ MEMOIR

          ☐ BIOGRAPHY ☐ OTHER _____

DATE STARTED: _____ DATE FINISHED: _____

RATING: ☆ ☆ ☆ ☆ ☆

INSPIRED ME TO LEARN ABOUT THESE SUBJECTS: _____

_____

_____

_____

_____

_____

_____

_____

_____

_____

_____

_____

_____

BEST MOVIE ADAPTATIONS OF BOOKS

BOOK I'D MOST WANT TO MAKE INTO A MOVIE

TITLE:

I'D CAST:

_____ AS _____

_____ AS _____

_____ AS _____

_____ AS _____

BOOKS I'D LIKE TO SEE MADE INTO ADAPTATIONS

MY LIST OF EXISTING MOVIE ADAPTATIONS TO SEE

TITLE: _____

AUTHOR: _____

DATE PUBLISHED: _____

CATEGORY: ☐ FICTION ☐ NONFICTION ☐ MEMOIR

☐ BIOGRAPHY ☐ OTHER _____

DATE STARTED: _____ DATE FINISHED: _____

RATING: ☆ ☆ ☆ ☆ ☆

INSPIRED ME TO LEARN ABOUT THESE SUBJECTS: _____

_____

_____

_____

_____

_____

_____

_____

_____

_____

_____

_____

_____

TITLE: _____

AUTHOR: _____

DATE PUBLISHED: _____

CATEGORY: ☐ FICTION ☐ NONFICTION ☐ MEMOIR

☐ BIOGRAPHY ☐ OTHER _____

DATE STARTED: _____ DATE FINISHED: _____

RATING: ☆ ☆ ☆ ☆ ☆

INSPIRED ME TO LEARN ABOUT THESE SUBJECTS: _____

_____

_____

_____

_____

_____

_____

_____

_____

_____

_____

_____

_____

_I declare after all there is no enjoyment like reading!
How much sooner one tires of anything than of a book! When I have
a house of my own, I shall be miserable if I have not an excellent library._

—Jane Austen

TITLE: _____

AUTHOR: _____

DATE PUBLISHED: _____

CATEGORY: ☐ FICTION ☐ NONFICTION ☐ MEMOIR

          ☐ BIOGRAPHY ☐ OTHER _____

DATE STARTED: _____ DATE FINISHED: _____

RATING: ☆ ☆ ☆ ☆ ☆

INSPIRED ME TO LEARN ABOUT THESE SUBJECTS: _____

_____

_____

_____

_____

_____

_____

_____

_____

_____

_____

_____

_____

TITLE: _____

AUTHOR: _____

DATE PUBLISHED: _____

CATEGORY: ☐ FICTION ☐ NONFICTION ☐ MEMOIR

☐ BIOGRAPHY ☐ OTHER _____

DATE STARTED: _____ DATE FINISHED: _____

RATING: ☆ ☆ ☆ ☆ ☆

INSPIRED ME TO LEARN ABOUT THESE SUBJECTS: _____

_____

_____

_____

_____

_____

_____

_____

_____

_____

_____

_____

_____

READING TREES

Made me want to learn more about these subjects

Made me want to
read these other books by
different authors

Made me want to read these
other books by the same author

BOOK

Made me want to
read these other books by
different authors

Made me want to learn more about these subjects

BOOK

Made me want to read these
other books by the same author

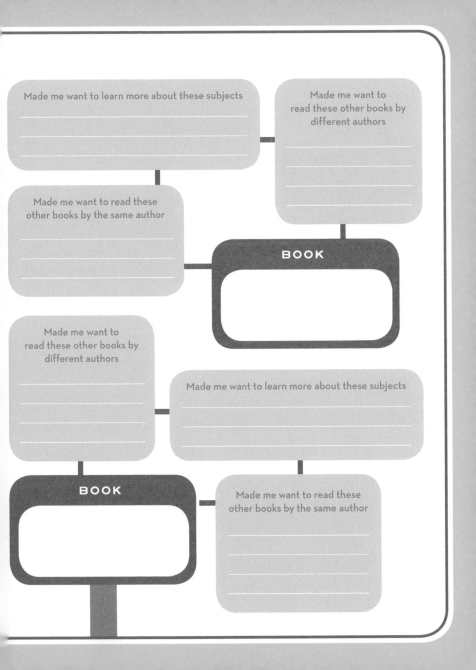

Made me want to learn more about these subjects

Made me want to
read these other books by
different authors

Made me want to read these
other books by the same author

BOOK

Made me want to
read these other books by
different authors

Made me want to learn more about these subjects

BOOK

Made me want to read these
other books by the same author

PULITZER PRIZE WINNERS (1948–PRESENT)

- ☐ 2013 _____
- ☐ 2012 _____
- ☐ 2011 _____
- ☐ 2010 _____
- ☐ 2009 *Olive Kitteridge,* Elizabeth Strout
- ☐ 2008 *The Brief Wondrous Life of Oscar Wao,* Junot Diaz
- ☐ 2007 *The Road,* Cormac McCarthy
- ☐ 2006 *March,* Geraldine Brooks
- ☐ 2005 *Gilead,* Marilynne Robinson
- ☐ 2004 *The Known World,* Edward P. Jones
- ☐ 2003 *Middlesex,* Jeffrey Eugenides
- ☐ 2002 *Empire Falls,* Richard Russo
- ☐ 2001 *The Amazing Adventures of Kavalier & Clay,* Michael Chabon
- ☐ 2000 *Interpreter of Maladies,* Jhumpa Lahiri
- ☐ 1999 *The Hours,* Michael Cunningham
- ☐ 1998 *American Pastoral,* Philip Roth
- ☐ 1997 *Martin Dressler: The Tale of an American Dreamer,* Steven Millhauser
- ☐ 1996 *Independence Day,* Richard Ford
- ☐ 1995 *The Stone Diaries,* Carol Shields
- ☐ 1994 *The Shipping News,* E. Annie Proulx
- ☐ 1993 *A Good Scent from a Strange Mountain,* Robert Olen Butler
- ☐ 1992 *A Thousand Acres,* Jane Smiley
- ☐ 1991 *Rabbit at Rest,* John Updike
- ☐ 1990 *The Mambo Kings Play Songs of Love,* Oscar Hijuelos
- ☐ 1989 *Breathing Lessons,* Anne Tyler
- ☐ 1988 *Beloved,* Toni Morrison
- ☐ 1987 *A Summons to Memphis,* Peter Taylor
- ☐ 1986 *Lonesome Dove,* Larry McMurtry
- ☐ 1985 *Foreign Affairs,* Alison Lurie
- ☐ 1984 *Ironweed,* William Kennedy
- ☐ 1983 *The Color Purple,* Alice Walker
- ☐ 1982 *Rabbit Is Rich,* John Updike
- ☐ 1981 *A Confederacy of Dunces,* John Kennedy Toole

- ☐ 1980 **The Executioner's Song,** Norman Mailer
- ☐ 1979 **The Stories of John Cheever,** John Cheever
- ☐ 1978 **Elbow Room,** James Alan McPherson
- ☐ 1977 **(No Award)**
- ☐ 1976 **Humboldt's Gift,** Saul Bellow
- ☐ 1975 **The Killer Angels,** Michael Shaara
- ☐ 1974 **(No Award)**
- ☐ 1973 **The Optimist's Daughter,** Eudora Welty
- ☐ 1972 **Angle of Repose,** Wallace Stegner
- ☐ 1971 **(No Award)**
- ☐ 1970 **Collected Stories,** Jean Stafford
- ☐ 1969 **House Made of Dawn,** N. Scott Momaday
- ☐ 1968 **The Confessions of Nat Turner,** William Styron
- ☐ 1967 **The Fixer,** Bernard Malamud
- ☐ 1966 **Collected Stories,** Katherine Anne Porter
- ☐ 1965 **The Keepers of the House,** Shirley Ann Grau
- ☐ 1964 **(No Award)**
- ☐ 1963 **The Reivers,** William Faulkner
- ☐ 1962 **The Edge of Sadness,** Edwin O'Connor
- ☐ 1961 **To Kill a Mockingbird,** Harper Lee
- ☐ 1960 **Advise and Consent,** Allen Drury
- ☐ 1959 **The Travels of Jaimie McPheeters,** Robert Lewis Taylor
- ☐ 1958 **A Death in the Family,** James Agee
- ☐ 1957 **(No Award)**
- ☐ 1956 **Andersonville,** MacKinlay Kantor
- ☐ 1955 **A Fable,** William Faulkner
- ☐ 1954 **(No Award)**
- ☐ 1953 **The Old Man and the Sea,** Ernest Hemingway
- ☐ 1952 **The Caine Mutiny,** Herman Wouk
- ☐ 1951 **The Town,** Conrad Richter
- ☐ 1950 **The Way West,** A. B. Guthrie
- ☐ 1949 **Guard of Honor,** James Gould Cozzens
- ☐ 1948 **Tales of the South Pacific,** James A. Michener

MAN BOOKER PRIZE FOR FICTION (1969–PRESENT)

- [ ] 2013 ────────────────────────────
- [ ] 2012 ────────────────────────────
- [ ] 2011 ────────────────────────────
- [ ] 2010 ────────────────────────────
- [ ] 2009 ────────────────────────────
- [ ] 2008 *The White Tiger,* Aravind Adiga
- [ ] 2007 *The Gathering,* Anne Enright
- [ ] 2006 *The Inheritance of Loss,* Kiran Desai
- [ ] 2005 *The Sea,* John Banville
- [ ] 2004 *The Line of Beauty,* Alan Hollinghurst
- [ ] 2003 *Vernon God Little,* DBC Pierre
- [ ] 2002 *Life of Pi,* Yann Martel
- [ ] 2001 *True History of the Kelly Gang,* Peter Carey
- [ ] 2000 *The Blind Assassin,* Margaret Atwood
- [ ] 1999 *Disgrace,* J. M. Coetzee
- [ ] 1998 *Amsterdam,* Ian McEwan
- [ ] 1997 *The God of Small Things,* Arundhati Roy
- [ ] 1996 *Last Orders,* Graham Swift
- [ ] 1995 *The Ghost Road,* Pat Barker
- [ ] 1994 *How Late It Was, How Late,* James Kelman
- [ ] 1993 *Paddy Clarke Ha Ha Ha,* Roddy Doyle
- [ ] 1992 *The English Patient,* Michael Ondaatje, and *Sacred Hunger,* Barry Unsworth
- [ ] 1991 *The Famished Road,* Ben Okri
- [ ] 1990 *Possession: A Romance,* A. S. Byatt
- [ ] 1989 *The Remains of the Day,* Kazuo Ishiguro
- [ ] 1988 *Oscar and Lucinda,* Peter Carey
- [ ] 1987 *Moon Tiger,* Penelope Lively
- [ ] 1986 *The Old Devils,* Kingsley Amis
- [ ] 1985 *The Bone People,* Keri Hulme
- [ ] 1984 *Hotel du Lac,* Anita Brookner
- [ ] 1983 *Life & Times of Michael K,* J. M. Coetzee
- [ ] 1982 *Schindler's Ark,* Thomas Keneally
- [ ] 1981 *Midnight's Children,* Salman Rushdie
- [ ] 1980 *Rites of Passage,* William Golding
- [ ] 1979 *Offshore,* Penelope Fitzgerald

- [ ] 1978 *The Sea, The Sea,* Iris Murdoch
- [ ] 1977 *Staying On,* Paul Scott
- [ ] 1976 *Saville,* David Storey
- [ ] 1975 *Heat and Dust,* Ruth Prawer Jhabvala
- [ ] 1974 *The Conservationist,* Nadine Gordimer, and *Holiday,* Stanley Middleton
- [ ] 1973 *The Siege of Krishnapur,* J. G. Farrell
- [ ] 1972 *G.,* John Berger
- [ ] 1971 *In a Free State,* V. S. Naipaul
- [ ] 1970 *The Elected Member,* Bernice Rubens
- [ ] 1969 *Something to Answer For,* P. H. Newby

NATIONAL BOOK AWARD FOR FICTION
(1950–PRESENT)

- [ ] 2013 _____
- [ ] 2012 _____
- [ ] 2011 _____
- [ ] 2010 _____
- [ ] 2009 _____
- [ ] 2008 *Shadow Country,* Peter Matthiessen
- [ ] 2007 *Tree of Smoke,* Denis Johnson
- [ ] 2006 *The Echo Maker,* Richard Powers
- [ ] 2005 *Europe Central,* William T. Vollmann
- [ ] 2004 *The News from Paraguay,* Lily Tuck
- [ ] 2003 *The Great Fire,* Shirley Hazzard
- [ ] 2002 *Three Junes,* Julia Glass
- [ ] 2001 *The Corrections,* Jonathan Franzen
- [ ] 2000 *In America,* Susan Sontag
- [ ] 1999 *Waiting,* Ha Jin
- [ ] 1998 *Charming Billy,* Alice McDermott
- [ ] 1997 *Cold Mountain,* Charles Frazier
- [ ] 1996 *Ship Fever and Other Stories,* Andrea Barrett
- [ ] 1995 *Sabbath's Theater,* Philip Roth
- [ ] 1994 *A Frolic of His Own,* William Gaddis
- [ ] 1993 *The Shipping News,* E. Annie Proulx
- [ ] 1992 *All the Pretty Horses,* Cormac McCarthy

- ☐ 1956 *Ten North Frederick,* John O'Hara
- ☐ 1955 *A Fable,* William Faulkner
- ☐ 1954 *The Adventures of Augie March,* Saul Bellow
- ☐ 1953 *Invisible Man,* Ralph Ellison
- ☐ 1952 *From Here to Eternity,* James Jones
- ☐ 1951 *The Collected Stories of William Faulkner,* William Faulkner
- ☐ 1950 *The Man with the Golden Arm,* Nelson Algren

NATIONAL BOOK CRITICS CIRCLE AWARD FOR FICTION (1975–PRESENT)

- ☐ 2013 ———————————————————————————
- ☐ 2012 ———————————————————————————
- ☐ 2011 ———————————————————————————
- ☐ 2010 ———————————————————————————
- ☐ 2009 ———————————————————————————
- ☐ 2008 **2666,** Roberto Bolaño
- ☐ 2007 *The Brief Wondrous Life of Oscar Wao,* Junot Diaz
- ☐ 2006 *The Inheritance of Loss,* Kiran Desai
- ☐ 2005 *The March,* E. L. Doctorow
- ☐ 2004 *Gilead,* Marilynne Robinson
- ☐ 2003 *The Known World,* Edward P. Jones
- ☐ 2002 *Atonement,* Ian McEwan
- ☐ 2001 *Austerlitz,* W. G. Sebald
- ☐ 2000 *Being Dead,* Jim Crace
- ☐ 1999 *Motherless Brooklyn,* Jonathan Lethem
- ☐ 1998 *The Love of a Good Woman,* Alice Munro
- ☐ 1997 *The Blue Flower,* Penelope Fitzgerald
- ☐ 1996 *Women in Their Beds,* Gina Berriault
- ☐ 1995 *Mrs. Ted Bliss,* Stanley Elkin
- ☐ 1994 *The Stone Diaries,* Carol Shields
- ☐ 1993 *A Lesson Before Dying,* Ernest J. Gaines
- ☐ 1992 *All the Pretty Horses,* Cormac McCarthy
- ☐ 1991 *A Thousand Acres,* Jane Smiley
- ☐ 1990 *Rabbit at Rest,* John Updike
- ☐ 1989 *Billy Bathgate,* E. L. Doctorow

- ☐ 1988 **The Middleman and Other Stories,** Bharati Mukherjee
- ☐ 1987 **The Counterlife,** Philip Roth
- ☐ 1986 **Kate Vaiden,** Reynolds Price
- ☐ 1985 **The Accidental Tourist,** Anne Tyler
- ☐ 1984 **Love Medicine,** Louise Erdrich
- ☐ 1983 **Ironweed,** William Kennedy
- ☐ 1982 **George Mills,** Stanley Elkin
- ☐ 1981 **Rabbit Is Rich,** John Updike
- ☐ 1980 **The Transit of Venus,** Shirley Hazzard
- ☐ 1979 **The Year of the French,** Thomas Flanagan
- ☐ 1978 **The Stories of John Cheever,** John Cheever
- ☐ 1977 **Song of Solomon,** Toni Morrison
- ☐ 1976 **October Light,** John Gardner
- ☐ 1975 **Ragtime,** E. L. Doctorow

PEN/FAULKNER AWARD FOR FICTION
(1981—PRESENT)

- ☐ 2013 _____
- ☐ 2012 _____
- ☐ 2011 _____
- ☐ 2010 _____
- ☐ 2009 **Netherland,** Joseph O'Neill
- ☐ 2008 **The Great Man,** Kate Christensen
- ☐ 2007 **Everyman,** Philip Roth
- ☐ 2006 **The March,** E. L. Doctorow
- ☐ 2005 **War Trash,** Ha Jin
- ☐ 2004 **The Early Stories, 1953—1975,** John Updike
- ☐ 2003 **The Caprices,** Sabina Murray
- ☐ 2002 **Bel Canto,** Ann Patchett,
- ☐ 2001 **The Human Stain,** Philip Roth
- ☐ 2000 **Waiting,** Ha Jin
- ☐ 1999 **The Hours,** Michael Cunningham
- ☐ 1998 **The Bear Comes Home,** Rafi Zabor
- ☐ 1997 **Women in Their Beds,** Gina Berriault
- ☐ 1996 **Independence Day,** Richard Ford

HEMINGWAY FOUNDATION/PEN AWARD
(1976–PRESENT)

THE MODERN LIBRARY: 100 BEST NOVELS

The Board's List

- ☐ *The Way of All Flesh,* Samuel Butler
- ☐ *Nineteen Eighty-four,* George Orwell
- ☐ *I, Claudius,* Robert Graves
- ☐ *To the Lighthouse,* Virginia Woolf
- ☐ *An American Tragedy,* Theodore Dreiser
- ☐ *The Heart Is a Lonely Hunter,* Carson McCullers
- ☐ *Slaughterhouse-Five,* Kurt Vonnegut
- ☐ *Invisible Man,* Ralph Ellison
- ☐ *Native Son*, Richard Wright
- ☐ *Henderson the Rain King,* Saul Bellow
- ☐ *Appointment in Samarra,* John O'Hara
- ☐ *U.S.A. (trilogy),* John Dos Passos
- ☐ *Winesburg, Ohio,* Sherwood Anderson
- ☐ *A Passage to India,* E. M. Forster
- ☐ *The Wings of the Dove,* Henry James
- ☐ *The Ambassadors,* Henry James
- ☐ *Tender Is the Night,* F. Scott Fitzgerald
- ☐ *The Studs Lonigan Trilogy,* James T. Farrell
- ☐ *The Good Soldier,* Ford Madox Ford
- ☐ *Animal Farm,* George Orwell
- ☐ *The Golden Bowl,* Henry James
- ☐ *Sister Carrie,* Theodore Dreiser
- ☐ *A Handful of Dust,* Evelyn Waugh
- ☐ *As I Lay Dying,* William Faulkner
- ☐ *All the King's Men,* Robert Penn Warren
- ☐ *The Bridge of San Luis Rey,* Thornton Wilder
- ☐ *Howards End,* E. M. Forster
- ☐ *Go Tell It on the Mountain,* James Baldwin
- ☐ *The Heart of the Matter,* Graham Greene
- ☐ *Lord of the Flies,* William Golding
- ☐ *Deliverance,* James Dickey
- ☐ *A Dance to the Music of Time (series),* Anthony Powell
- ☐ *Point Counter Point,* Aldous Huxley
- ☐ *The Sun Also Rises,* Ernest Hemingway
- ☐ *The Secret Agent,* Joseph Conrad
- ☐ *Nostromo,* Joseph Conrad

- [ ] *The Rainbow,* D. H. Lawrence
- [ ] *Women in Love,* D. H. Lawrence
- [ ] *Tropic of Cancer,* Henry Miller
- [ ] *The Naked and the Dead,* Norman Mailer
- [ ] *Portnoy's Complaint,* Philip Roth
- [ ] *Pale Fire,* Vladimir Nabokov
- [ ] *Light in August,* William Faulkner
- [ ] *On the Road,* Jack Kerouac
- [ ] *The Maltese Falcon,* Dashiell Hammett
- [ ] *Parade's End,* Ford Madox Ford
- [ ] *The Age of Innocence,* Edith Wharton
- [ ] *Zuleika Dobson,* Max Beerbohm
- [ ] *The Moviegoer,* Walker Percy
- [ ] *Death Comes for the Archbishop,* Willa Cather
- [ ] *From Here to Eternity,* James Jones
- [ ] *The Wapshot Chronicles,* John Cheever
- [ ] *The Catcher in the Rye,* J. D. Salinger
- [ ] *A Clockwork Orange,* Anthony Burgess
- [ ] *Of Human Bondage,* W. Somerset Maugham
- [ ] *Heart of Darkness,* Joseph Conrad
- [ ] *Main Street,* Sinclair Lewis
- [ ] *The House of Mirth,* Edith Wharton
- [ ] *The Alexandria Quartet,* Lawrence Durell
- [ ] *A High Wind in Jamaica,* Richard Hughes
- [ ] *A House for Mr. Biswas,* V. S. Naipaul
- [ ] *The Day of the Locust,* Nathanael West
- [ ] *A Farewell to Arms,* Ernest Hemingway
- [ ] *Scoop,* Evelyn Waugh
- [ ] *The Prime of Miss Jean Brodie,* Muriel Spark
- [ ] *Finnegans Wake,* James Joyce
- [ ] *Kim,* Rudyard Kipling
- [ ] *A Room with a View,* E. M. Forster
- [ ] *Brideshead Revisited,* Evelyn Waugh
- [ ] *The Adventures of Augie March,* Saul Bellow
- [ ] *Angle of Repose,* Wallace Stegner
- [ ] *A Bend in the River,* V. S. Naipaul

- [ ] *The Death of the Heart,* Elizabeth Bowen
- [ ] *Lord Jim,* Joseph Conrad
- [ ] *Ragtime,* E. L. Doctorow
- [ ] *The Old Wives' Tale,* Arnold Bennett
- [ ] *The Call of the Wild,* Jack London
- [ ] *Loving,* Henry Green
- [ ] *Midnight's Children,* Salman Rushdie
- [ ] *Tobacco Road,* Erskine Caldwell
- [ ] *Ironweed,* William Kennedy
- [ ] *The Magus,* John Fowles
- [ ] *Wide Sargasso Sea,* Jean Rhys
- [ ] *Under the Net,* Iris Murdoch
- [ ] *Sophie's Choice,* William Styron
- [ ] *The Sheltering Sky,* Paul Bowles
- [ ] *The Postman Always Rings Twice,* James M. Cain
- [ ] *The Ginger Man,* J. P. Donleavy
- [ ] *The Magnificent Ambersons,* Booth Tarkington

The Readers' List

- [ ] *Atlas Shrugged,* Ayn Rand
- [ ] *The Fountainhead,* Ayn Rand
- [ ] *Battlefield Earth,* L. Ron Hubbard
- [ ] *The Lord of the Rings,* J. R. R. Tolkien
- [ ] *To Kill a Mockingbird,* Harper Lee
- [ ] *Nineteen Eighty-four,* George Orwell
- [ ] *Anthem,* Ayn Rand
- [ ] *We the Living,* Ayn Rand
- [ ] *Mission Earth,* L. Ron Hubbard
- [ ] *Fear,* L. Ron Hubbard
- [ ] *Ulysses,* James Joyce
- [ ] *Catch-22,* Joseph Heller
- [ ] *The Great Gatsby,* F. Scott Fitzgerald
- [ ] *Dune,* Frank Herbert
- [ ] *The Moon Is a Harsh Mistress,* Robert A. Heinlein
- [ ] *Stranger in a Strange Land,* Robert A. Heinlein
- [ ] *A Town Like Alice,* Nevil Shute

- [ ] *Brave New World,* Aldous Huxley
- [ ] *The Catcher in the Rye,* J. D. Salinger
- [ ] *Animal Farm,* George Orwell
- [ ] *Gravity's Rainbow,* Thomas Pynchon
- [ ] *The Grapes of Wrath,* John Steinbeck
- [ ] *Slaughterhouse Five,* Kurt Vonnegut
- [ ] *Gone with the Wind,* Margaret Mitchell
- [ ] *Lord of the Flies,* William Golding
- [ ] *Shane,* Jack Schaefer
- [ ] *Trustee from the Toolroom,* Nevil Shute
- [ ] *A Prayer for Owen Meany,* John Irving
- [ ] *The Stand,* Stephen King
- [ ] *The French Lieutenant's Woman,* John Fowles
- [ ] *Beloved,* Toni Morrison
- [ ] *The Worm Ouroboros,* E. R. Eddison
- [ ] *The Sound and the Fury,* William Faulkner
- [ ] *Lolita,* Vladimir Nabokov
- [ ] *Moonheart,* Charles de Lint
- [ ] *Absalom, Absalom!* William Faulkner
- [ ] *Of Human Bondage,* W. Somerset Maugham
- [ ] *Wise Blood,* Flannery O'Connor
- [ ] *Under The Volcano,* Malcolm Lowry
- [ ] *Fifth Business,* Robertson Davies
- [ ] *Someplace to Be Flying,* Charles de Lint
- [ ] *On the Road,* Jack Kerouac
- [ ] *Heart of Darkness,* Joseph Conrad
- [ ] *Yarrow,* Charles de Lint
- [ ] *At the Mountains of Madness,* H. P. Lovecraft
- [ ] *One Lonely Night,* MIckey Spillane
- [ ] *Memory and Dream,* Charles de Lint
- [ ] *To the Lighthouse,* Virginia Woolf
- [ ] *The Moviegoer,* Walker Percy
- [ ] *Trader,* Charles de Lint
- [ ] *The Hitchhiker's Guide to the Galaxy,* Douglas Adams
- [ ] *The Heart Is a Lonely Hunter,* Carson McCullers
- [ ] *The Handmaid's Tale,* Margaret Atwood
- [ ] *Blood Meridian,* Cormac McCarthy

- [ ] *A Clockwork Orange,* Anthony Burgess
- [ ] *On the Beach,* Nevil Shute
- [ ] *A Portrait of the Artist as a Young Man,* James Joyce
- [ ] *Greenmantle,* Charles de Lint
- [ ] *Ender's Game,* Orson Scott Card
- [ ] *The Little Country,* Charles de Lint
- [ ] *The Recognitions,* William Gaddis
- [ ] *Starship Troopers,* Robert A. Heinlein
- [ ] *The Sun Also Rises,* Ernest Hemingway
- [ ] *The World According to Garp,* John Irving
- [ ] *Something Wicked This Way Comes,* Ray Bradbury
- [ ] *The Haunting of Hill House,* Shirley Jackson
- [ ] *As I Lay Dying,* William Faulkner
- [ ] *Tropic of Cancer,* Henry Miller
- [ ] *Invisible Man,* Ralph Ellison
- [ ] *The Wood Wife,* Terri Windling
- [ ] *The Magus,* John Fowles
- [ ] *The Door into Summer,* Robert A. Heinlein
- [ ] *Zen and the Art of Motorcycle Maintenance,* Robert Pirsig
- [ ] *I, Claudius,* Robert Graves
- [ ] *The Call of the Wild,* Jack London
- [ ] *At Swim-Two-Birds,* Flann O'Brien
- [ ] *Fahrenheit 451,* Ray Bradbury
- [ ] *Arrowsmith,* Sinclair Lewis
- [ ] *Watership Down,* Richard Adams
- [ ] *Naked Lunch,* William S. Burroughs
- [ ] *The Hunt for Red October,* Tom Clancy
- [ ] *Guilty Pleasures,* Laurell K. Hamilton
- [ ] *The Puppet Masters,* Robert A. Heinlein
- [ ] *It,* Stephen King
- [ ] *V.,* Thomas Pynchon
- [ ] *Double Star,* Robert A. Heinlein
- [ ] *Citizen of the Galaxy* Robert A. Heinlein
- [ ] *Brideshead Revisited,* Evelyn Waugh
- [ ] *Light in August,* William Faulkner
- [ ] *One Flew over the Cuckoo's Nest,* Ken Kesey

- [ ] *A Farewell to Arms,* Ernest Hemingway
- [ ] *The Sheltering Sky,* Paul Bowles
- [ ] *Sometimes a Great Notion,* Ken Kesey
- [ ] *My Ántonia,* Willa Cather
- [ ] *Mulengro,* Charles de Lint
- [ ] *Suttree,* Cormac McCarthy
- [ ] *Mythago Wood,* Robert Holdstock
- [ ] *Illusions,* Richard Bach
- [ ] *The Cunning Man,* Robertson Davies
- [ ] *The Satanic Verses,* Salman Rushdie

BBC: TOP 100 READS

- [ ] *The Lord of the Rings,* J. R. R Tolkien
- [ ] *Pride and Prejudice,* Jane Austen
- [ ] *His Dark Materials,* Philip Pullman
- [ ] *The Hitchhiker's Guide to the Galaxy,* Douglas Adams
- [ ] *Harry Potter and the Goblet of Fire,* J. K. Rowling
- [ ] *To Kill a Mockingbird,* Harper Lee
- [ ] *Winnie-the-Pooh,* A. A. Milne
- [ ] *Nineteen Eighty-four,* George Orwell
- [ ] *The Lion, the Witch and the Wardrobe,* C. S. Lewis
- [ ] *Jane Eyre,* Charlotte Brontë
- [ ] *Catch-22,* Joseph Heller
- [ ] *Wuthering Heights,* Emily Brontë
- [ ] *Birdsong,* Sebastian Faulks
- [ ] *Rebecca,* Daphne du Maurier
- [ ] *The Catcher in the Rye,* J. D. Salinger
- [ ] *The Wind in the Willows,* Kenneth Grahame
- [ ] *Great Expectations,* Charles Dickens
- [ ] *Little Women,* Louisa May Alcott
- [ ] *Captain Corelli's Mandolin,* Louis de Bernières
- [ ] *War and Peace,* Leo Tolstoy
- [ ] *Gone with the Wind,* Margaret Mitchell
- [ ] *Harry Potter and the Philosopher's Stone,* J. K. Rowling
- [ ] *Harry Potter and the Chamber of Secrets,* J. K. Rowling

- [ ] *Harry Potter and the Prisoner of Azkaban,* J. K. Rowling
- [ ] *The Hobbit,* J. R. R. Tolkien
- [ ] *Tess of the d'Urbervilles,* Thomas Hardy
- [ ] *Middlemarch,* George Eliot
- [ ] *A Prayer for Owen Meany,* John Irving
- [ ] *The Grapes of Wrath,* John Steinbeck
- [ ] *Alice's Adventures in Wonderland,* Lewis Carroll
- [ ] *The Story of Tracy Beaker,* Jacqueline Wilson
- [ ] *One Hundred Years of Solitude,* Gabriel García Márquez
- [ ] *The Pillars of the Earth,* Ken Follett
- [ ] *David Copperfield,* Charles Dickens
- [ ] *Charlie and the Chocolate Factory,* Roald Dahl
- [ ] *Treasure Island,* Robert Louis Stevenson
- [ ] *A Town Like Alice,* Nevil Shute
- [ ] *Persuasion,* Jane Austen
- [ ] *Dune,* Frank Herbert
- [ ] *Emma,* Jane Austen
- [ ] *Anne of Green Gables,* L. M. Montgomery
- [ ] *Watership Down,* Richard Adams
- [ ] *The Great Gatsby,* F. Scott Fitzgerald
- [ ] *The Count of Monte Cristo,* Alexandre Dumas
- [ ] *Brideshead Revisited,* Evelyn Waugh
- [ ] *Animal Farm,* George Orwell
- [ ] *A Christmas Carol,* Charles Dickens
- [ ] *Far from the Madding Crowd,* Thomas Hardy
- [ ] *Goodnight Mister Tom,* Michelle Magorian
- [ ] *The Shell Seekers,* Rosamunde Pilcher
- [ ] *The Secret Garden,* Frances Hodgson Burnett
- [ ] *Of Mice and Men,* John Steinbeck
- [ ] *The Stand,* Stephen King
- [ ] *Anna Karenina,* Leo Tolstoy
- [ ] *A Suitable Boy,* Vikram Seth
- [ ] *The BFG,* Roald Dahl
- [ ] *Swallows and Amazons,* Arthur Ransome
- [ ] *Black Beauty,* Anna Sewell
- [ ] *Artemis Fowl,* Eoin Colfer

- [ ] *Crime and Punishment,* Fyodor Dostoyevsky
- [ ] *Noughts and Crosses,* Malorie Blackman
- [ ] *Memoirs of a Geisha,* Arthur Golden
- [ ] *A Tale of Two Cities,* Charles Dickens
- [ ] *The Thorn Birds,* Colleen McCollough
- [ ] *Mort,* Terry Pratchett
- [ ] *The Magic Faraway Tree,* Enid Blyton
- [ ] *The Magus,* John Fowles
- [ ] *Good Omens,* Terry Pratchett and Neil Gaiman
- [ ] *Guards! Guards!* Terry Pratchett
- [ ] *Lord of the Flies,* William Golding
- [ ] *Perfume,* Patrick Süskind
- [ ] *The Ragged Trousered Philanthropists,* Robert Tressell
- [ ] *Night Watch,* Terry Pratchett
- [ ] *Matilda,* Roald Dahl
- [ ] *Bridget Jones's Diary,* Helen Fielding
- [ ] *The Secret History,* Donna Tartt
- [ ] *The Woman in White,* Wilkie Collins
- [ ] *Ulysses,* James Joyce
- [ ] *Bleak House,* Charles Dickens
- [ ] *Double Act,* Jacqueline Wilson
- [ ] *The Twits,* Roald Dahl
- [ ] *I Capture the Castle,* Dodie Smith
- [ ] *Holes,* Louis Sachar
- [ ] *Gormenghast,* Mervyn Peake
- [ ] *The God of Small Things*, Arundhati Roy
- [ ] *Vicky Angel,* Jacqueline Wilson
- [ ] *Brave New World,* Aldous Huxley
- [ ] *Cold Comfort Farm,* Stella Gibbons
- [ ] *Magician,* Raymond E. Feist
- [ ] *On the Road,* Jack Kerouac
- [ ] *The Godfather,* Mario Puzo
- [ ] *The Clan of the Cave Bear,* Jean M. Auel
- [ ] *The Colour of Magic,* Terry Pratchett
- [ ] *The Alchemist,* Paulo Coelho
- [ ] *Katherine,* Anya Seton

- [ ] *Kane and Abel,* Jeffrey Archer
- [ ] *Love in the Time of Cholera,* Gabriel García Márquez
- [ ] *Girls in Love,* Jacqueline Wilson
- [ ] *The Princess Diaries,* Meg Cabot
- [ ] *Midnight's Children,* Salman Rushdie

TIME MAGAZINE: TOP 100 NOVELS
(ALPHABETICAL ORDER)

- [ ] *The Adventures of Augie March,* Saul Bellow
- [ ] *All the King's Men,* Robert Penn Warren
- [ ] *American Pastoral,* Philip Roth
- [ ] *An American Tragedy,* Theodore Dreiser
- [ ] *Animal Farm,* George Orwell
- [ ] *Appointment in Samarra,* John O'Hara
- [ ] *Are You There God? It's Me, Margaret,* Judy Blume
- [ ] *The Assistant,* Bernard Malamud
- [ ] *At Swim-Two-Birds,* Flann O'Brien
- [ ] *Atonement,* Ian McEwan
- [ ] *Beloved,* Toni Morrison
- [ ] *The Berlin Stories,* Christopher Isherwood
- [ ] *The Big Sleep,* Raymond Chandler
- [ ] *The Blind Assassin,* Margaret Atwood
- [ ] *Blood Meridian,* Cormac McCarthy
- [ ] *Brideshead Revisited,* Evelyn Waugh
- [ ] *The Bridge of San Luis Rey,* Thornton Wilder
- [ ] *Call It Sleep,* Henry Roth
- [ ] *Catch-22,* Joseph Heller
- [ ] *The Catcher in the Rye,* J. D. Salinger
- [ ] *A Clockwork Orange,* Anthony Burgess
- [ ] *The Confessions of Nat Turner,* William Styron
- [ ] *The Corrections,* Jonathan Franzen
- [ ] *The Crying of Lot 49,* Thomas Pynchon
- [ ] *A Dance to the Music of Time,* Anthony Powell
- [ ] *The Day of the Locust,* Nathanael West
- [ ] *Death Comes for the Archbishop,* Willa Cather

- [ ] *A Death in the Family,* James Agee
- [ ] *The Death of the Heart,* Elizabeth Bowen
- [ ] *Deliverance,* James Dickey
- [ ] *Dog Soldiers,* Robert Stone
- [ ] *Falconer,* John Cheever
- [ ] *The French Lieutenant's Woman,* John Fowles
- [ ] *The Golden Notebook,* Doris Lessing
- [ ] *Go Tell It on the Mountain,* James Baldwin
- [ ] *Gone With the Wind,* Margaret Mitchell
- [ ] *The Grapes of Wrath,* John Steinbeck
- [ ] *Gravity's Rainbow,* Thomas Pynchon
- [ ] *The Great Gatsby,* F. Scott Fitzgerald
- [ ] *A Handful of Dust,* Evelyn Waugh
- [ ] *The Heart Is a Lonely Hunter,* Carson McCullers
- [ ] *The Heart of the Matter,* Graham Greene
- [ ] *Herzog,* Saul Bellow
- [ ] *A House for Mr. Biswas,* V. S. Naipaul
- [ ] *Housekeeping,* Marilynne Robinson
- [ ] *I, Claudius,* Robert Graves
- [ ] *Infinite Jest,* David Foster Wallace
- [ ] *Invisible Man,* Ralph Ellison
- [ ] *Light in August,* William Faulkner
- [ ] *The Lion, the Witch and the Wardrobe,* C. S. Lewis
- [ ] *Lolita,* Vladimir Nabokov
- [ ] *Lord of the Flies,* William Golding
- [ ] *The Lord of the Rings,* J. R. R. Tolkien
- [ ] *Loving,* Henry Green
- [ ] *Lucky Jim,* Kingsley Amis
- [ ] *The Man Who Loved Children,* Christina Stead
- [ ] *Midnight's Children,* Salman Rushdie
- [ ] *Money,* Martin Amis
- [ ] *The Moviegoer,* Walker Percy
- [ ] *Mrs. Dalloway,* Virginia Woolf
- [ ] *Naked Lunch,* William Burroughs
- [ ] *Native Son,* Richard Wright
- [ ] *Neuromancer,* William Gibson
- [ ] *Never Let Me Go,* Kazuo Ishiguro

- [ ] *Nineteen Eighty-four,* George Orwell
- [ ] *On the Road,* Jack Kerouac
- [ ] *One Flew over the Cuckoo's Nest,* Ken Kesey
- [ ] *The Painted Bird,* Jerzy Kosinski
- [ ] *Pale Fire,* Vladimir Nabokov
- [ ] *A Passage to India,* E. M. Forster
- [ ] *Play It As It Lays,* Joan Didion
- [ ] *Portnoy's Complaint,* Philip Roth
- [ ] *Possession,* A. S. Byatt
- [ ] *The Power and the Glory,* Graham Greene
- [ ] *The Prime of Miss Jean Brodie,* Muriel Spark
- [ ] *Rabbit, Run,* John Updike
- [ ] *Ragtime,* E. L. Doctorow
- [ ] *The Recognitions,* William Gaddis
- [ ] *Red Harvest,* Dashiell Hammett
- [ ] *Revolutionary Road,* Richard Yates
- [ ] *The Sheltering Sky,* Paul Bowles
- [ ] *Slaughterhouse-Five,* Kurt Vonnegut
- [ ] *Snow Crash,* Neal Stephenson
- [ ] *The Sot-Weed Factor,* John Barth
- [ ] *The Sound and the Fury,* William Faulkner
- [ ] *The Sportswriter,* Richard Ford
- [ ] *The Spy Who Came in from the Cold,* John le Carré
- [ ] *The Sun Also Rises,* Ernest Hemingway
- [ ] *Their Eyes Were Watching God,* Zora Neale Hurston
- [ ] *Things Fall Apart,* Chinua Achebe
- [ ] *To Kill a Mockingbird,* Harper Lee
- [ ] *To the Lighthouse,* Virginia Woolf
- [ ] *Tropic of Cancer,* Henry Miller
- [ ] *Ubik,* Philip K. Dick
- [ ] *Under the Net,* Iris Murdoch
- [ ] *Under the Volcano,* Malcolm Lowry
- [ ] *Watchmen,* Alan Moore and Dave Gibbons
- [ ] *White Noise,* Don DeLillo
- [ ] *White Teeth,* Zadie Smith
- [ ] *Wide Sargasso Sea,* Jean Rhys

OPRAH'S BOOK CLUB PICKS (1996–PRESENT)

- ☐ 2013 _____
- ☐ 2012 _____
- ☐ 2011 _____
- ☐ 2010 _____
- ☐ 2009 _____

2008

- ☐ *The Story of Edgar Sawtelle,* David Wroblewski
- ☐ *A New Earth,* Eckhart Tolle

2007

- ☐ *The Pillars of the Earth,* Ken Follett
- ☐ *Love in the Time of Cholera,* Gabriel García Márquez
- ☐ *Middlesex,* Jeffrey Eugenides
- ☐ *The Road,* Cormac McCarthy
- ☐ *The Measure of a Man,* Sidney Poitier

2006

- ☐ *Night,* Elie Wiesel

2005

- ☐ *A Million Little Pieces,* James Frey
- ☐ *Light in August,* William Faulkner
- ☐ *The Sound and the Fury,* William Faulkner
- ☐ *As I Lay Dying,* William Faulkner

2004

- ☐ *The Good Earth,* Pearl S. Buck
- ☐ *Anna Karenina,* Leo Tolstoy
- ☐ *The Heart Is a Lonely Hunter,* Carson McCullers
- ☐ *One Hundred Years of Solitude,* Gabriel García Márquez

2003

- ☐ *Cry, the Beloved Country,* Alan Paton
- ☐ *East of Eden,* John Steinbeck

2002

- ☐ *Sula,* Toni Morrison
- ☐ *Fall on Your Knees,* Ann-Marie MacDonald

2001

- ☐ *A Fine Balance,* Rohinton Mistry
- ☐ *The Corrections,* Jonathan Franzen
- ☐ *Cane River,* Lalita Tademy
- ☐ *Stolen Lives: Twenty Years in a Desert Jail,* Malika Oufkir
- ☐ *Icy Sparks,* Gwyn Hyman Rubio
- ☐ *We Were the Mulvaneys,* Joyce Carol Oates

2000

- ☐ *House of Sand and Fog,* Andre Dubus III
- ☐ *Drowning Ruth,* Christina Schwarz
- ☐ *Open House,* Elizabeth Berg
- ☐ *The Poisonwood Bible,* Barbara Kingsolver
- ☐ *While I Was Gone,* Sue Miller
- ☐ *The Bluest Eye,* Toni Morrison
- ☐ *Back Roads,* Tawni O'Dell
- ☐ *Daughter of Fortune,* Isabel Allende
- ☐ *Gap Creek,* Robert Morgan

1999

- ☐ *A Map of the World,* Jane Hamilton
- ☐ *Vinegar Hill,* A. Manette Ansay
- ☐ *River, Cross My Heart,* Breena Clarke
- ☐ *Tara Road,* Maeve Binchy
- ☐ *Mother of Pearl,* Melinda Haynes
- ☐ *White Oleander,* Janet Fitch
- ☐ *The Pilot's Wife,* Anita Shreve
- ☐ *The Reader,* Bernhard Schlink
- ☐ *Jewel,* Bret Lott

1998

- [ ] *Where the Heart Is,* Billie Letts
- [ ] *Midwives,* Chris Bohjalian
- [ ] *What Looks Like Crazy on an Ordinary Day,* Pearl Cleage
- [ ] *I Know This Much Is True,* Wally Lamb
- [ ] *Breath, Eyes, Memory,* Edwidge Danticat
- [ ] *Black and Blue,* Anna Quindlen
- [ ] *Here on Earth,* Alice Hoffman
- [ ] *Paradise,* Toni Morrison

1997

- [ ] *The Best Way to Play,* Bill Cosby
- [ ] *The Treasure Hunt,* Bill Cosby

- [ ] *The Meanest Thing to Say,* Bill Cosby
- [ ] *A Virtuous Woman,* Kaye Gibbons
- [ ] *Ellen Foster,* Kaye Gibbons
- [ ] *A Lesson Before Dying,* Ernest J. Gaines
- [ ] *Songs in Ordinary Time,* Mary McGarry Morris
- [ ] *The Heart of a Woman,* Maya Angelou
- [ ] *The Rapture of Canaan,* Sheri Reynolds
- [ ] *Stones from the River,* Ursula Hegi
- [ ] *She's Come Undone,* Wally Lamb

1996

- [ ] *The Book of Ruth,* Jane Hamilton
- [ ] *Song of Solomon,* Toni Morrison
- [ ] *The Deep End of the Ocean,* Jacquelyn Mitchard

ADVENTURE FAVORITES

- [ ] *Alice's Adventures in Wonderland,* Lewis Carroll
- [ ] *Around the World in Eighty Days,* Jules Verne
- [ ] *Gulliver's Travels,* Jonathan Swift
- [ ] *The Island of Doctor Moreau,* H. G. Wells
- [ ] *Journey to the Center of the Earth,* Jules Verne
- [ ] *The Jungle Book,* Rudyard Kipling
- [ ] *Robinson Crusoe,* Daniel DeFoe
- [ ] *Swiss Family Robinson,* Johann D. Wyss
- [ ] *Time Machine,* H. G. Wells
- [ ] *Treasure Island,* Robert Louis Stevenson
- [ ] *20,000 Leagues under the Sea,* Jules Verne

EPIC NOVEL FAVORITES

- [ ] *Atlas Shrugged,* Ayn Rand
- [ ] *The Brothers Karamazov,* Fyodor Dostoevsky
- [ ] *Dr. Zhivago,* Boris Pasternak
- [ ] *Don Quixote,* Miguel de Cervantes

- ☐ *Grapes of Wrath,* John Steinbeck
- ☐ *Lord of the Rings,* J. R. R. Tolkien
- ☐ *One Hundred Years of Solitude,* Gabriel García Márquez
- ☐ *Ulysses,* James Joyce
- ☐ *V.,* Thomas Pynchon
- ☐ *War and Peace,* Leo Tolstoy

GOTHIC/HORROR FAVORITES

- ☐ *The Castle of Otranto,* Horace Walpole
- ☐ *Dracula,* Bram Stoker
- ☐ *Frankenstein: Or the Modern Prometheus,* Mary Shelley
- ☐ *Jane Eyre,* Charlotte Brontë
- ☐ *The Mystery of Edwin Drood,* Charles Dickens
- ☐ *The Picture of Dorian Gray,* Oscar Wilde
- ☐ *The Strange Case of Dr. Jekyll and Mr. Hyde,* Robert Louis Stevenson
- ☐ *The Turn of the Screw,* Henry James
- ☐ *Wuthering Heights,* Emily Brontë

GRAPHIC NOVEL FAVORITES

- ☐ *Black Hole,* Charles Burns
- ☐ *Bone,* Jeff Smith
- ☐ *Ghostworld,* Daniel Clowes
- ☐ *Maus: A Survivor's Tale,* Art Spiegelman
- ☐ *Persepolis,* Marjane Satrapi
- ☐ *Sandman,* Neil Gaiman
- ☐ *V for Vendetta,* Alan Moore
- ☐ *Watchmen,* Alan Moore and Dave Gibbons

INTERNATIONAL FAVORITES

- ☐ *Bonjour Tristesse,* Françoise Sagan (France)
- ☐ *The Cairo Trilogy (Palace Walk, Palace of Desire, Sugar Street),* Naguib Mahfouz (Egypt)
- ☐ *Cry, the Beloved Country,* Alan Paton (South Africa)

- [ ] *Disgrace,* J. M. Coetzee (South Africa)
- [ ] *Dona Flor and Her Two Husbands,* Jorge Amado (Brazil)
- [ ] *The God of Small Things,* Arundhati Roy (India)
- [ ] *The House of Spirits,* Isabel Allende (Chile)
- [ ] *Hunger,* Knut Hamsun (Norway)
- [ ] *The Leopard,* Giuseppe di Lampedusa (Italy)
- [ ] *Like Water for Chocolate*, Laura Esquivel (Mexico)
- [ ] *Maps,* Farah Nurrudin (Somalia)
- [ ] *Master and Margarita,* Mikhail Bulgakov (Russia)
- [ ] *My Name Is Red,* Orhan Pamuk (Turkey)
- [ ] *One Hundred Years of Solitude,* Gabriel García Márquez (Columbia)
- [ ] *Steppenwolf,* Hermann Hesse (Germany)
- [ ] *The Stranger,* Albert Camus (France)
- [ ] *Things Fall Apart,* Chinua Achebe (Nigeria)
- [ ] *The Tin Drum,* Günter Grass (Germany)
- [ ] *2666,* Robert Bolaño (Chile)
- [ ] *The Unbearable Lightness of Being,* Milan Kundera (Czech Republic)
- [ ] *The Wind-Up Bird Chronicle,* Haruki Murakami (Japan)

MYSTERY/DETECTIVE FICTION FAVORITES

- [ ] *And Then There Were None,* Agatha Christie
- [ ] *The Big Sleep,* Raymond Chandler
- [ ] *The Dalton Case,* Ross MacDonald
- [ ] *Devil in a Blue Dress,* Walter Mosley
- [ ] *Gaudy Night,* Dorothy Sayers
- [ ] *The Maltese Falcon,* Dashiell Hammett
- [ ] *The Moonstone,* Wilkie Collins
- [ ] *The Murders in the Rue Morgue,* Edgar Allan Poe
- [ ] *The Postman Always Rings Twice,* James M. Cain
- [ ] *A Study in Scarlet,* Sir Arthur Conan Doyle

ROMANCE FAVORITES

- ☐ *Gone with the Wind,* Margaret Mitchell
- ☐ *Middlemarch,* George Eliot
- ☐ *Outlander,* Diana Gabaldon
- ☐ *Pride and Prejudice,* Jane Austen
- ☐ *Rebecca,* Daphne du Maurier
- ☐ *A Room with a View,* E. M. Forster
- ☐ *Vanity Fair,* William Makepeace Thackeray

SCIENCE FICTION FAVORITES

- ☐ *The Andromeda Strain,* Michael Crichton
- ☐ *Cat's Cradle,* Kurt Vonnegut
- ☐ *Ender's Game,* Orson Scott Card
- ☐ *Fahrenheit 451,* Ray Bradbury
- ☐ *Foundation,* Isaac Asimov
- ☐ *The Hitchhiker's Guide to the Galaxy,* Douglas Adams
- ☐ *I Am Legend,* Richard Matheron
- ☐ *Stranger in a Strange Land,* Robert A. Heinlein
- ☐ *War of the Worlds,* H. G. Wells
- ☐ *A Wrinkle in Time,* Madeleine L'Engle

SPY NOVEL FAVORITES

- ☐ *Ashenden, or The British Agent,* W. Somerset Maugham
- ☐ *The Bourne Identity,* Robert Ludlum
- ☐ *The Company,* Robert Littell
- ☐ *From Russia with Love,* Ian Fleming
- ☐ *Kim,* Rudyard Kipling
- ☐ *Our Man in Havana,* Graham Greene
- ☐ *The Scarlet Pimpernel,* Baroness Orczy
- ☐ *Six Days of the Condor,* James Grady
- ☐ *The Thirty-Nine Steps,* John Buchan
- ☐ *Tinker, Tailor, Soldier, Spy,* John le Carré

MY LIST OF BOOKS TO READ

Use these pages to plan your reading. Use the recommended reading lists if you're looking for inspiration.

MY LIST OF BOOKS TO READ

MY LIST OF BOOKS TO READ

AUTHOR TALKS

Authors I've seen read in person

AUTHOR: _____

WHAT HE/SHE READ: _____

WHERE: _____

NOTES: _____

_____

_____

_____

_____

_____

AUTHOR: _____

WHAT HE/SHE READ: _____

WHERE: _____

NOTES: _____

_____

_____

_____

_____

_____

AUTHOR: _____

WHAT HE/SHE READ: _____

WHERE: _____

NOTES: _____

_____

_____

_____

AUTHOR: _____

WHAT HE/SHE READ: _____

WHERE: _____

NOTES: _____

_____

_____

_____

AUTHOR: _____

WHAT HE/SHE READ: _____

WHERE: _____

NOTES: _____

_____

_____

AUTHOR TALKS

Authors I've seen read in person

AUTHOR: _____

WHAT HE/SHE READ: _____

WHERE: _____

NOTES: _____

_____

_____

_____

_____

_____

AUTHOR: _____

WHAT HE/SHE READ: _____

WHERE: _____

NOTES: _____

_____

_____

_____

_____

_____

_____

AUTHOR: _____

WHAT HE/SHE READ: _____

WHERE: _____

NOTES: _____

_____

_____

_____

AUTHOR: _____

WHAT HE/SHE READ: _____

WHERE: _____

NOTES: _____

_____

_____

_____

AUTHOR: _____

WHAT HE/SHE READ: _____

WHERE: _____

NOTES: _____

_____

_____

BORROWING AND LOANING RECORDS

Books I've borrowed from family or friends:

BOOK	FROM	DATE BORROWED	DATE RETURNED

Books friends or family have borrowed from me:

BOOK	TO	DATE BORROWED	DATE RETURNED

BOOK SOURCE ADDRESS BOOK

Addresses and contact information for my favorite book sources
(libraries and bookstores—chain, used, specialty, foreign, etc.)

NAME: _____

ADDRESS: _____

WEBSITE: _____

TELEPHONE: _____

NOTES: _____

_____

_____

_____

NAME: _____

ADDRESS: _____

WEBSITE: _____

TELEPHONE: _____

NOTES: _____

_____

_____

_____

NAME: _____

ADDRESS: _____

WEBSITE: _____

TELEPHONE: _____

NOTES: _____

_____

_____

_____

_____

_____

NAME: _____

ADDRESS: _____

WEBSITE: _____

TELEPHONE: _____

NOTES: _____

_____

_____

_____

_____

_____

BOOK SOURCE ADDRESS BOOK

NAME: _____

ADDRESS: _____

WEBSITE: _____

TELEPHONE: _____

NOTES: _____

_____

_____

_____

_____

_____

NAME: _____

ADDRESS: _____

WEBSITE: _____

TELEPHONE: _____

NOTES: _____

_____

_____

_____

_____